THE "R" EFFECT

HOW
NURTURING
RELATIONSHIPS
IS THE **KEY TO BOOSTING**
ANY **BUSINESS**

J. MICHAEL CAVITT

Author: J. Michael Cavitt
Title: The "R" Effect
ISBN: 978-1-927892-53-4
Category: BUSINESS & ECONOMICS/Customer Relations

Publisher:
Black Card Books™
Division of Gerry Robert Enterprises Inc.
Suite 214, 5-18 Ringwood Drive
Stouffville, Ontario
Canada, L4A 0N2
International Calling: 1-647-361-8577
www.blackcardbooks.com

THE "R" EFFECT

HOW
NURTURING
RELATIONSHIPS
IS THE **KEY TO BOOSTING**
ANY **BUSINESS**

J. MICHAEL CAVITT

TABLE OF CONTENTS

ACKNOWLEDGEMENTS

I want to thank everyone who has helped...Okay, here are some names that must be known:

Mark LeBlanc, smallbusinesssuccess.com, for starting this ball rolling.

Mary Carol Moore, marycarrollmoore.com, for showing me a little of what I didn't know about writing and directing me to a great writing tool, Scrivener, literatureandlatte.com.

Dara Beevas, wiseinkpub.com, for showing me more and answering questions.

Gerry Robert and Jean-Guy Francoeur, blackcardbooks.com, for encouraging me to follow through.

Providers of refuge: Will Ruff and Jeannie and Deryl Mitchell.

Providers of encouragement: While too many to name, I give a special thank you to everyone who has encouraged me in this work.

The people I interviewed, who are listed in the back, receive a thank you for the information they provided me. Listening to and reading the interviews multiple times have been most educational.

INTRODUCTION

WHO IS THE BOOK FOR?

If you are responsible for the results, directly or indirectly, of your sales team or you are a sales professional and concerned about your own results, then this book was written for you.

And you want to boost your business from where it is now to a new level.

WHAT'S THE PROBLEM?

Research shows that on average, 48% of sales professionals do not make a second contact with the prospect (see Table in the Appendix). From this, I can infer that if they do make a sale on the first contact, they won't follow-up to help the buyer become a customer.

First, this is throwing away money for both the company and the sales professional. Second, when no relationship exists or there is no record of it, when the sales professional leaves the company, information, relationships, and money are lost. It has been described to me as stealing from the company.

WHAT WILL YOU LEARN FROM READING THIS BOOK?

You will gain a deeper understanding of the importance of creating and nurturing relationships and trust to boost your business.

You will know the critical steps to creating an effective follow-through system for sales professionals: Systems for Strengthening Relationships™.

HOW WILL YOU BE BETTER OFF AFTER READING THIS BOOK?

You will have the information, which will help you to determine if you need to improve the relationship-building aspect of your client acquisition and retention plan. Or, said more simply, you will know if your sales force needs help creating and maintaining relationships to acquire and keep clients.

WHAT ARE THE THREE KEY POINTS OF THE BOOK?

1. Relationships are the key to boosting your business. Relationships are built by follow-up with customers and prospects.

No follow-up, no consistent results.

2. Effective follow-up creates and nurtures relationships and trust. Effective follow-up is maintained by systems of consistent communication that create and nurture relationships and trust.

No system, no consistent, effective follow-up.

Well-thought-out systems are mandatory for building outward-facing relationships for the business. In addition, some thought should also be given to inward-facing relationship building in organizations.

3. Consistent, effective use of systems creates and nurtures relationships and trust. Effective planning creates effective systems of communication.

No planning, no effective system.

The planning for the systems should be part of the larger planning process.

Systems, that maintain consistent communication, are the result of including them in a project plan, the operational business plan, and the strategic plan.

The nurturing of relationships and trust, both inward-facing and outward-facing, should be at least in the back of your mind for all planning. The question should be, "How is relationship building affected by the plan?"

WHY DID I WRITE THE BOOK?

A few years ago when I went back and reread Max Gunther's book, *The Luck Factor,* one trait of "lucky people" is they create and maintain a "spider web of contacts" I was reminded, both conceptually and visually by large piles of business cards on my desk, that I like the vast majority of people do not naturally create and maintain spider webs or networks of contacts.

I decided to help others and myself by focusing on the situation. This book is the result of that decision.

WHY DO INTERVIEWS?

I've always learned best by listening to others. So, I interviewed the people who are quoted in this book, as well as others, and learned a lot from them, as I hope you will.

The "What" and "Why"

The chapters in this section will give you information about what relationships in business are and why they are important because without this information, there is no reason to review your follow-up campaigns and systems.

You will read some of the answers I received to the five questions that I asked in my interviews. The interviewee is listed after each quote and the complete list with contact information is at the end of the book.

The questions explore different aspects of relationships in business and their impact on boosting business, as well as relationship building, in general.

Each chapter of this section starts with the question that I asked. The responses from the interviewees are generally verbatim.

I was occasionally asked to modify answers that might violate client confidentiality; however, the gist of the answers was preserved. Some of the answers were edited for clarity.

QUESTION 1

Coming from your position of _____ with _____, will you share with me how relationships and relationship building are viewed in your company/business?

REPLACES MARKETING

Ajay Mandal, IT Consultant and Business Owner

"Relationship building is especially important for small businesses like mine. I don't have a big budget. I must grow my business by nurturing relationships.

As the business owner and primary sales person for my business, I have focused on building relationships rather than knocking on doors. I've built strategic relationships with companies that are very complementary to my business. That way, I don't have to do mass marketing to acquire only one or two new clients.

So, relationships are very important to me. It's a two-way street. They bring the business and I subcontract with them or give them a commission. This gives them a financial stake which will encourage them to continue to bring business back to me.

It's very hard to keep a balance with only one or two referrals. You want to build some kind of incentive into the relationship that keeps nurturing that relationship."

RELATIONSHIPS ARE THE CORE

C. J. Hayden, Author and Coach

"So, I believe that relationships are really the core of building any kind of professional services business. For a professional in private practice, whether they're a consultant, coach, graphic designer, or an architect, if they're providing a professional service, relationships are at the heart of that service, both in terms of securing clients to begin with and staying in a relationship with those clients throughout the course of the service that they provide to them.

It's very different for a business that provides a product. When you provide a professional service, the relationship with the client is part of what is transacted. For that reason, relationships are even more important in this kind of business than in any other kind of business."

Michael: Okay, let me add a follow-on question to that. Why do you think that a significant percentage of the people that you're talking about don't pay attention to that?

C.J.: **"Fear**."

Michael: Okay, would you like to expand on that?

C.J.: "Yes, I will. You know, because of the fact that when you're providing a service, when you're in a service business, what you're really selling is you're selling yourself. I think the kind of rejection that people fear can be sometimes totally paralyzing. And I see so many people because a big part of what I do is advise and teach and coach people on how to market themselves. I see so many people who are unsuccessful at doing that because of the fact that their fear of rejection in that circumstance is so strong that they'll do almost anything to avoid actually putting themselves out there in such a way that they can be rejected. So they hide behind, for example, marketing methods that don't require them to put themselves out there. So they send out emails, they write letters, they put up a website, they don't talk to people. And by doing that, they're shooting themselves in the foot because they're not building the relationships necessary to get clients and to ultimately serve clients. But they're doing it because all of those things seem so much easier and less confronting than what's actually required to build a successful business."

THEY WANT BOTH

Chuck Palmer, Financial Services Regional Managing Director

It's absolutely critical. In the old days, we used to argue about whether a potential buyer or potential client was purchasing expertise or a relationship.

I look back at that and I realize it was a silly discussion because, quite frankly, our clients and potential clients want more.

They want both a high level of expertise and competency in this area, and a relationship.

Your role in that relationship is primarily that of a business advisor relationship. The relationship is also sometimes a personal relationship because clients want to have both and a good balance of both helps clients to feel that they're getting what they would like from their professional service provider."

LEVERAGE

Crystal Thies, "The LinkedIn Ninja"

"In my business, which is all about teaching people how to utilize LinkedIn for sales and business development, relationships are very important. Having some kind of a base-level relationship and being able to leverage those relationships to get you what it is you need and/or want for your own business.

Now, that being said, a lot of people read that wrong, meaning that leverage is taking advantage of people, and that's not the case. It's finding the right person by having the relationships to make introductions and open doors for you to move along the pathway towards where you're trying to get to.

It's not taking advantage because I always tell people that in building that relationship, you have to start by giving them something first. You can't ask for a favor before you've given them something and something hopefully that you've done proactively, not because they asked you to.

But it really is all about building the relationships so that you can open the right doors when *you need them to be open.*"

PERSPECTIVE

Dave Hubers, past President

"I would say relationships were one of the most critical parts of our business strategy.

Financial services businesses often are focused on transactions. In our case, we were focused on relationships. The key to building those relationships was 1) having financial advisors who understood and valued relationships and 2) doing financial planning so we understood the total financial picture of the client and made sure we were recommending products that would fit into his or her portfolio and help them meet their long-term objectives.

So, relationships were a key element to our strategy."

NOT BUSINESS TO BUSINESS (B2B), BUT PERSON TO PERSON (P2P)

Deb Brown, Client Retention Specialist

"Well, I think that people do not want to do business with a business. They want to do it with another person and so, that relationship is key. You can go, if you need to, and buy something and pick something up at a big box store and that's fine. But if you really need a service you want someone you can have a relationship with and you feel like you can trust them. Business gets done between people, so if you nurture those relationships then you're going to naturally see more business."

RELATIONSHIPS WITH THE AUDIENCE

Deirdre Van Nest, Professional Speaker, Coach

"My whole approach in teaching professionals how to create effective talks that really wow their audience and get other people to buy into their ideas is actually all about building relationships with your audience."

LONG-TERM, NOT TRANSACTIONAL

Jenny Foss, Job Search Strategist

"It's interesting because I have worked in two different worlds. I have ran a recruiting agency for almost a decade that serves corporate clients who are looking to fill an open position. So  essentially, we're headhunters. And in more recent years, we launched the second business which is the JobJenny.com. And that is more geared toward people making transitions in their careers or actively job seeking. And that's strategic consulting and job search support towards the same range.

So very tied together yet serving two different audiences because one is going right to a consumer and one is going to a business client.

In terms of the relationship factor, it's interesting that you mention that because my husband is a recruiter for a large global recruiting firm, and we had this very conversation this week.

Some in the recruitment industry, unfortunately, treat the relationship as a kind of a one-and-done. They go out for the kill. They find their match. They close that person and they collect their money and score.

He and I are both very different in our mindsets in that if you approach it from the long relationship-building standpoint, you might not, in the short-term, have the one-and-done successes that some of the differently-focused recruiters have. But from a long-term growth and trust standpoint, it just always works out so much better.

And interestingly, there is a lot turnover in the recruiting industry among headhunters I do believe that part of the reason why is they have been trained somehow to believe that this is a numbers game. It's just a number. And when we do that, sometimes you fail at building long-term relationships. And it's those relationships that are going to sustain you in any business but certainly in the recruiting industry.

Now, from the standpoint of being a consultant to those in transition, so job seekers and people wanting to make career move, it is extraordinarily important to build trust with this audience in particular because a lot of those who are coming to us are now at a stage where they're proactively thinking about nipping the situation in the bud at the front end. It's awesome they're coming to us because the things that they've been trying in the name of job search and trying that move, they're not working.

And so, they're struggling and they're stressed. And in a lot of instances, they're running out of money, they're starting to panic, their self-esteem is taking a hit, and so at that stage where we come into the picture, they are absolutely needing to feel like they have somebody who not only is qualified to support their needs, but also that they can trust because they're going to be laying a lot out there for us in terms of personal information and fears that we need to take good care of.

And I think that part of the growth of JobJenny.com, which has been rapid over the last three years, is coming from our hard and fast belief that this is not a transactional deal. This is not just, 'Here, let's us rewrite your resume. There you go. Goodbye.' It's about having a relationship with the people that we serve and really understanding where they're coming from and where they're trying to go.

And we're fortunate. We did an analysis recently. More than 60% of our business for our resume service and our consulting service, more than 60% comes from referrals from happy clients.

I mean I'd like to think that we're doing something right in terms of the relationship. And I think it's proof. That's proof that taking the time and really demonstrating what we call the 'you care' factor, it pays off. I mean it just pays off. This is not a transactional relationship, or it if is, people don't want it to be.

They wanted to feel like they have somebody in their court. They want to feel like somebody is there right alongside of them, cheerleading for them, and helping them find a different way."

RELATIONSHIPS, INTROVERTS, AND HEALTH

Lynette Crane, Introvert Coach

"Well, my view is that they are extraordinarily important. They're fundamental, really, since my emphasis is working with introverts and low-functioning introverts isolate themselves. They have what I call 'introvert baggage.' They suffer. I'm sure their health suffers because of it, too.

So, I believe that developing and maintaining relationships is an absolutely fundamental thing in life. It can reduce your fear, for

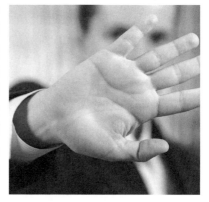

example. And introverts typically live with a lot of anxiety, a lot of fear. Well, the lower-functioning ones do. I can't think of anything you could accomplish in life that you couldn't accomplish much better and much more joyously if you have a network of supportive relationships to build up. That's my viewpoint."

MAINTAIN IT

Matt Nye, Insurance Agent

"The people you can build a relationship with, they'll be your client for a lifetime.

Once you've established that, you've just got to maintain it. You just have to treat them like people.

You just have to care about what actually happens with them and be concerned about their well being, making sure that they are going to be successful, as well. And they will make you successful, in turn."

INTERNAL RELATIONSHIPS FOSTER COLLABORATION

Michael Lane, Company president and former Vice President at Cargill

❝In the context of Cargill, the focus of the need for effective relationships is the ability to reach across the organization and get things done or to get answers to questions or to provide movement for projects that get stalled or initiatives that get derailed for some reason or another. If you had a relationship with someone in another area of Cargill that you could place a phone call or have lunch with, you can say, 'I need you to bless this. Here's what's going on.'

At a fundamental level, there are three things for me that strengthen relationships. Number one is trust, two is authenticity, and three is communication.

If you have authenticity with somebody across the organization and they have found your dealing with them in the past have been truthful and honest and above board and there is a level of trust there, then that request for help or for some assistance will get rewarded."

MISSED OPPORTUNITIES

Steve Callender, Coach and Trainer

"About as fundamental as air. When I have maintained relationships, it's been very productive and rewarding. When I have let relationships go, and I have more often than I would like to even admit to myself, nothing happens.

It's a matter of missed opportunities. It's a matter of having to create things from scratch where they could've been developed on based on a relationship. It just makes everything much more difficult when relationships are not maintained."

SHOPPING RELATIONSHIPS

Susie Dircks, COO of a Recruiting Company

"When we talk to organizations and clients about why we want to do business with them and when we work with prospects, we're considering that we shop for clients just like clients shop for an agency. And if at any point in the process we believe that relationships aren't going to be important or equally significant on the client side, it may beg the question, 'Are we working with the client that it makes sense on both sides?' So for us it's important for our client to recognize the value in working with a team of people that, first of all doesn't change. You're going to have some turnover, but you're going to have a team of people who really understand your business. They understand your business and are able to separate it out from all the other clients that we might work with.

So it's key to not only how we 'land an account,' but also how we continue to build and grow and build our depth of a partnership into an account. Because one thing that's important for us is once we get going on an account that we're doing business with, we don't want to stop at that one relationship and one partnership. We then want to go what we say 'deep and wide' into that client's account. And that, I believe, is done through the building of relationships."

SEE THE BIG PICTURE

Teresa Thomas, Director of Woman's Networking Organization

"Relationships are viewed in a big-picture way where you're not looking for a transactional relationship, but building a relationship that goes through the world in different ways and doesn't necessarily mean that what I give to you comes back equally to me. It also is about realizing that we all have our own network and that the connections we make and build trust with  often times will lead to referrals and building credibility, expertise, learning from each other, but that the people we meet aren't necessarily our potential clients. They may be, but it's about building that relationship first."

RELATIONSHIP WITH YOURSELF

Theresa Rose, Speaker, Author, Mentor

"Every single time that I get on stage and share a keynote with an organization, it has an underpinning of how someone can improve or grow in connection in relationship with their world. And that world could be their job, their coworkers, their family members, their romantic relationship, and, ultimately, the relationship with themselves.

That is really where I play to help people establish a healthier relationship with themselves. And when they do that, then every other relationship flourishes, every other relationship grows.

When they have established a healthier, more powerful and more forgiving relationship with themselves.

That's what also comes through in my writing and in my mentoring of people."

LEADERSHIP

Tom Laughlin, Executive Coach

"The fact is leadership can only be done in a relationship. There is no real ability to lead. You can give instructions, but there is no ability to lead without a relationship.

And the relationship has a significant impact on your ability to do that.

So, relationships of all types and sizes are fundamental to leadership and to foundations of leadership. And having the ability to work within different types of relationships and having them be effective is a big part of what leadership development is."

ANOTHER BIG BRAIN AT THE TABLE

Stephanie Laitala-Rupp, Owner of Bookkeeping and CFO Service

"Well, in our company, it is critical. I mean, we handle one of the things that brings people the most stress: money. So it's all about the relationship.

And we work with business owners. They open the kimono. There's no option, right? I mean, we know when there's no money for payroll. We know when it gets tough. We know when there's extra money and they get to take it home. I mean, we see the whole spectrum of either physical health or physical sickness, if you will. And it gets personal and private, and it doesn't get more stressful than money, frankly.

And so, we have to be able to have an incredibly detailed, trustworthy, intimate relationship with our clients.

Our first core value is that we treat our client's business as if it was our own. We use words like 'we' and 'ours.' 'We need to write a check for ...' 'We're not going to make payroll.' Never, 'You're not going to make payroll.' We take it personally.

Part of that is because of who we are as individuals. That's who I hire: people who would treat it personally and feel as if it's their business, not just a client's business. But part of it is intentional, making sure that business owners understand that it's not a 'you.' It's an 'us.' It's not 'you, me.' It's an 'us.' And that helps strengthen the relationships.

I'm not going to go through all those core values, but the first two really deal with I think sort of the relationship aspect. Our second core value is we are your sharing expert.

We understand that our clients may or may not be sophisticated or comfortable with money and financial statements and that whole thing. And they turn to us for calm advice, calm guidance, solid advice.

We absolutely make sure that we are another big brain at the table. We don't underestimate the importance of that. Another big brain that has their best interest at heart. Someone who isn't so immersed in the trees that they can't see the forest. And I think that's why they turn to us again and again for moral support and that voice of reason."

INTERNAL RELATIONSHIPS

Tom O'Neill, Company President

"I think there're many facets of relationship building that are integral to our organization. I'd have to start with internally, our employees.

I think we've got almost 500 employees now. We do custom, web, and mobile development. So the biggest relationships internally are, right now, between the people who generate new business, our sales team, and the people who get the work done, our software development and design teams.

And, man, that's been a constant challenge over the last 10 years as we've grown. I think it is for many businesses. Sales and fulfillment are kind of naturally opposed, but we've concentrated heavily on building relationships between those teams and I think we're doing a pretty darn good job of it. I'm quite proud of the relationships and the level of trust that those relationships bring between the two teams.

So I think it starts there because if we can't get along internally, it's really hard to maintain external relationships.

And, you know, it's not all 'Kumbaya' around here. There are some real problems. We're running a fast-growing business, but we've, very pragmatically, broken down some of the would-be barriers by just understanding that we're all human beings here. We all have feelings. We all have difference approaches and objectives. And if we talk to each other, if we trust each other, and if we work together as a team, it just makes it a heck of a lot easier to solve these problems we're faced with every day. That's kind of our internal look at it."

LIKED VS. RESPECTED

Scott Plum, Sales Trainer

"I 've seen an importance of relationships versus transactional selling; however, sales people can get very comfortable with maintaining a relationship and thinking that they are nurturing a sale or working with the prospect to become a client when in reality, they just are becoming better friends.

There is a difference between being liked and being respected. And often sales people get caught up in being liked and maintaining a relationship, but not taking it to the next level and earning the respect of the prospect.

In a business relationship, the goal is to convert the conversation into a close and the prospect to a client.

Respect should be the goal, not maintaining a relationship."

Writer's Note: I've included definitions because in reading Scott's quote, I needed them to help me appreciate what he said.

Definitions:

Relationship: The way in which two or more people are connected, or the state of being connected.

Friendship: The emotions or conduct of friends; the state of being friends.

Friend: A person whom one knows and with whom one has a bond of mutual affection, typically exclusive of sexual or family relations.

Trust: Firm belief in the reliability, truth, ability, or strength of someone or something.

Respect: A feeling of deep admiration for someone or something elicited by their abilities, qualities, or achievements.

Like: Find agreeable, enjoyable, or satisfactory.

Source: Dictionary Version 2.2.3 (118.5) Apple, Inc

TRENDS IN RELATIONSHIP BUILDING

Tom Downing, Realtor

"The type of work that I did, at Turning Point Group, is specifically about building relationships, so let me answer on three levels. The first started historically when we started the business 13 years ago.

People did not understand full how important the relationship was in building your business. I think people talked about it and some people did it, but certain industries are certainly further along than others.

But almost no one was putting serious dollars and serious energy behind sort of relationship management other than maybe a CRM program that usually failed because they got some high-tech answer to it. They tried to implement it in the company and because they didn't really understand the quantum of why they were doing it, what they were trying to achieve, and how they were going to use it, it was a great idea, but they would fail. I think most of them failed throughout most of the 90's.

Then you started to see a change when people really realized, especially when the economy got tighter, that it was a lot cheaper, as we all know, to keep our customers and to get more from current relationships than we do from new ones.

So, all of a sudden, you started to see people like Chief Customer Officers, Chief Relationship Officers. People started to put some energy behind it, and that's what we do. Turning Point Group was really in an industry that had not gotten so far along.

That was all started back then, but now you start to see relationships that have become much broader, like, in hospitals.

How do you develop a relationship with a group of customers who are fundamentally trying to keep themselves out of your facility? How do you develop relationship? Or how do you show importance to executives?

What's the financial impact of developing relationships in a non-frequency environment, let's say, where we're not trying to repeat them. We're trying to keep them out, but when they do come, how do we make sure that it's the most beneficial, both financially and for outcomes, for both parties?"

QUESTION 2

What are your personal thoughts on strengthening relationships and trust?

BUYING YOU REQUIRES TRUST

Allen Vaysberg, IT Entrepreneur

"With me, those two things go together because if you don't have trust, you're not going to have a relationship.

Relationship to me is not just an ability of people to communicate with one another because we communicate with others all the time. We say, 'Hello' and 'How are you?' and go on our merry way. That is not a relationship to me.

Without trust, you will not be able to take on the words that I would say to you and take them as something that would be internalized. So, unless there is a trust, then the people will not have a relationship with you.

And for me, in this business that I'm launching or the previous enterprises that we've built from ground up, it was all about relationships. Whether it's in-person relationships or it is over the Internet, in this new business, it's all about trust.

The reason why people bought from us or they followed us was purely because of trust. So, in order to built that relationship, you must have trust and you must understand that the other person is not going to be buying anything from you.

They are buying you. If they believe in who you are, what you stand for, and what you're trying to do, and that you have their best interest at heart, then they will deal with you. Otherwise, it doesn't matter."

BUILDING TRUST AND DESTROYING TRUST

Barbara Sanderson, Coach

"I think that's a really complicated subject. In fact, I do a lot of teaching and coaching around trust and how to build trust. I think trust is a complex set of interactions.

There are things that each one of us do to build trust, behaviors and mindsets. And there are behaviors and mindsets that destroy trust.

In any relationship, the trust quotient is kind of the plus versus the minus, and I think nobody is completely trustworthy. I think we all have areas where we're trustworthy and areas where we're not."

DO YOU CARE?

Chuck Palmer, Financial Services Regional Managing Director

" It may sound trite, but people want to know if you really care. They want to know if you really care about them, if you really care about their business, or if you're trying to just sell them something. That's not a relationship most people want to have.

When someone feels that you care about them, that you are willing to invest a big part of yourself and your business acumen with them, they begin to trust you. And of course, hopefully, that advice starts working well with them. That to me is why you nurture relationships and build trust.

Show them that you care about them holistically, not just selling the next job."

TASK TRUST VS. INTERPERSONAL TRUST

Debbie Magnuson, Coach, Facilitator, and Consultant

" My personal thoughts. Well, I'm a completely relationship-oriented person, so that's hard for me to even ponder. I'd rather gear towards trust for just a moment.

One of the big ah-ha's that I've had is understanding the difference between task trust and interpersonal trust, and how one goes about strengthening that. Task trust is, 'Do I trust you that you know how to do the task in front of you? Do I trust that you can run those reports or that you can do what I asked you to do from a technical standpoint?' And that's one level, you know?

And then interpersonal trust is, 'Do I believe you have my back? Do I trust that you care about me as a person, at a deeper level?' That's an entirely different thing.

Understanding that differentiation has been very helpful in my work with teens inside organizations to help them realize that just being able to do the doing isn't really what builds strong relationships that are there when we most need them, right? That it's that deeper level of relationships, of relationship trust, interpersonal trust that's really vital."

LONELY WITHOUT RELATIONSHIPS

Deirdre Van Nest, Professional Speaker, Coach

"Relationships are everything in life. It is a very lonely existence without them. What's the point of life without relationships?

At the end of the day, that's kind of what it boils down to. That's what it's all about."

TRUST COMES FIRST

Denise Lee Yohn, Brand Building Expert

"To me, trust comes first and then that's the basis for a relationship. And what I have discovered or the approach that I use is that to trust first and then expect trust back rather than going into a relationship kind of skeptical and waiting for the other person to kind of prove their worth of my trust or my investment in the relationships.

I really try to put my trust out there first and make it known to people that I usually look for the good in people, expect good things from people, and respect people, and want to engage in a trust-based relationship. And then over time, hopefully they come to see that that is really the way that I operate, and hopefully they come to trust me in return."

THE ONLY WAY

James Olsen, Attorney

"The only way to strengthen trust is to build relationships."

INTENTION?

Kit Welchin, Speaker and Trainer

"I think the most critical part of it is to really know what your long-term intention is."

PEER RELATIONSHIP

Lisa Magnotta, Company President

"The relationships that I look to build are those that can provide me the insight to move my company forward.

I joined Allied Executives back in November. And even though I have only been going to only four or five of my monthly group meetings, I walk away each time with a renewed sense of affirmation in my role, as well as a feeling that I've got partners out there that even though they're not in my business or even in my industry, they know exactly what I'm going through.

The discussions we have in group meetings are real. They're not abstract and they're not all about variants. Even something as basic as, 'I think one of my employees might be stealing from me,' and we talk about that.

And we can say that honestly and freely without fear of retribution, where my colleagues aren't going to look on me like,

'Whoa, don't you have your controls in place?' They're like, 'No, we understand because we've been through this.' It's almost like going to a therapist where you can just open up and talk about anything and get some real, valid input because these people have been through this.

Often times, they can provide that perspective that might be different from mine because the whole adage that 'you can't see the forest for the trees' is truly what it's like when you've been running your business for a while. You can't think outside the box like you used to. So, by talking and building relationships with other business owners or other presidents of companies, you're able to glean some of that perspective outside that is truly objective and immensely valuable."

LISTENING

Michael Lane, Company president and Former Vice President at Cargill

" In some ways it comes down to a very basic thing and that is listening.

If someone comes to you and you can convey the ability to listen to them and they sense the sincerity in your listening, trust flows from that interaction. And 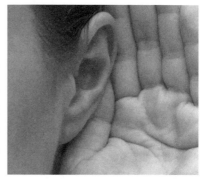 over time, those interactions with other people build into an even greater amount of trust. But if you don't listen to people, if it's just a passing attention to what their critical interests are, it is so apparent. And we know it and have experienced both sides of that."

WHO WILL YOU WALK THE JOURNEY WITH?

Stephanie Laitala-Rupp, Owner of Bookkeeping and CFO Service

" Well, it's all about the relationship frankly. I mean, it's never really what you know. It's more of who you know and who's willing to walk the journey with you and stand up for you.

In the personal services businesses, especially one like Owl, we handle people's money. We get 80% of our business by referrals and that's because of our relationships with those people. They trust us to give great service to the people that they refer to us.

They stick their neck out for us because they trust us.

So, personally, it's about who you walk the journey with, frankly.

So, it's all about relationships."

LONELINESS SUCKS

Steve Lear, Financial Services Company President

" I think I don't know anybody who likes to be lonely for a long period of time. Loneliness is very debilitating. Even for those who are extreme introverts, being alone is not a positive thing on a long-term basis.

So what it means then, is all of us need to focus on trying to create relationships because the option sucks."

CORE VALUES

Steve Wilcox, Coach and Consultant

"Well, I would again refer back to a personal belief of looking at core values. I am involved in a couple of key nonprofit and volunteer settings that have probably framed who I am as much as anything in my life.

One is Rotary International and the 4-Way Test. And the second is scouting, the Scout Law and Oath and so on.

When you are aligned with adults and young people who share those same beliefs, then that relationship is on solid foundation right from the get go. And so, that for me is almost an immediate trust, and I probably tend to give more trust at the outset than I should because I'm of the opinion that although trust is earned, you have not caused me to believe that I can't trust you until you do something that causes me to believe that I can't trust you.

So, therefore, trust is something that I believe in right from the earliest moment until a person causes me to believe otherwise. A couple of those core values and beliefs like I outlined with scouting and with Rotary come with an immediate trust level. That's how I gauge my relationships and navigate life."

WE DON'T HAVE MUCH IN LIFE, BUT RELATIONSHIPS

Tim Brands, Company President

"Yeah, that's a very interesting question for me personally. I mean, I'm a natural introvert. I am probably more analytical thinking if you think of the Strengths Finder™. I've got things like deliberative, analytical, and those types of things. You know, even from a Kolbe Index™, I initiate with follow-through.

You look at who I am personally. I'm not naturally a people person. Over the years, I've really developed a keen understanding of that.

I think it's John Maxwell who, when he started out, he wanted to make a difference. And then he realized he couldn't do it alone, so he wanted to make a difference with people. And then he realized that not everyone wanted to do what he wanted to do, so he wanted to make a difference with people who wanted to make a difference. It just continues to go on.

I think just the more I lead a team, the more I do consulting, even things like our work in Guatemala, which is a very people-oriented culture. As my kids get older, the longer I've been married, we really don't have much in this life that can be counted on and is really enduring other than relationships."

PREPARATION: A STORY

Tom O'Neill, Company President

❝I'll tell you a story that really inspired me, and I've been trying to model this for quite some time. There's a guy by the name of Fred Senn. He co-founded Fallon, the ad agency here in town [Twin Cities]. So, Pat Fallon and Fred Senn co-founded Fallon years ago, and I had the opportunity to get breakfast with Fred probably four years ago.

I asked him for a quick meeting. I wanted to learn about how to run a big business and how to maintain strong cultures, and Fallon had been known for their culture. And I reached out by kind of just asking if I, you know, could sit down with him for 15 minutes and talk about it. He graciously accepted.

He said, 'You know what? Let's do breakfast instead.' And so I met him downtown for breakfast, and I was really excited.

And I had met him through a personal connection, so we went and had breakfast. I was a little bit nervous. This guy is the millionaire co-founder of the most famous ad agency in the Twin Cities and arguably one of the top agencies in the world.

So, I sat down with Fred, and we began to talk. I had questions prepared and stuff like that, but I was fumbling a bit. And he pulled out a moleskin book that he had, and it was marked with a page. He opened up to that page, and at the top of the page it was my name, my company's name, my wife's name, and a list of questions that he had prepared for me.

And I was just floored. I couldn't believe it.

I said, 'Wow'

He had found out through the personal connection about my wife's name, then he prepared some questions. I can't remember what they were, but the point is that he took the time to really be thoughtful about how the interaction would go with me.

We got breakfast, and he knew what my wife's name was. I thought that was the coolest thing in the world. I was honored to meet him. The last thing I expected was for him to prepare for that meeting, so I've kind of carried that with me ever since I met Fred.

I've tried to follow his lead, so whether it's an external meeting, if I have time to prepare, or if it's someone internally here in the company. If I happen to have a meeting on a project level with a programmer or designer, I'll do my homework ahead of time, and I'll make sure I know the programmer's name.

I will make sure I knew when they started, who their manager was."

QUESTION 3

Can you give me more information on how you have found relationship building helpful or not helpful with boosting business?

TAKING TIME

Alyssa Granlund, Marketing Consultant

❝ I run a large women's networking organization called eWomenNetwork, and I run a chapter in the Minneapolis-St. Paul area.

It's wonderful because I get the opportunity to meet everybody in the room. I get to help people really get connected and meet other people. So, it's a natural thing for me to do that.

I've always been kind of interested in meeting new people and that's really fun. One of the things that I've noticed is some people become a part of the organization and they look at it as, 'How can I make a quick sale? How can I find somebody who wants to buy my product or my service?' They don't put in the time to build the relationships, you know? So there's a few people that are like that.

The people in the group that come to the group and put in the time to get to know each other and to build the relationships and see how they can help other people rather than just see how people can help them, those people really thrive in the group.

So, it's just been really interesting for me to watch in the last few years, how that goes, you know? It's just kind of a little group to see it work, but it's amazing when people do spend the time, how much more their businesses thrive.

I saw that, too, in my practice. When I work with people because I get very involved in their business and I get involved in getting to know them, not just as a client, but as a friend, because we're talking about how to build their business. Then, I become a really important part of their decision making because that relationship is so valued and trusted, but it definitely takes time to do that."

WORD OF MOUTH

Amy Scott, Coach and Editor

❝ I can't say if there's any way that it has not been helpful. I think the bulk of my work comes from relationships and word of mouth.

I think that the significant piece of it is the more people I know and the more people that I have quality relationships with or people who think well of me no matter how well they know me, it can only be good for business."

YOU GET A SECOND CHANCE

Dave Larson, Credit Union President

"I think where I find it helpful is that when you have a relationship, you get a second chance. We have 185,000 members and we have 500 employees.

You know what happens sometimes? We make a mistake. There are times when a member comes in and sits across the desk for me and they'll be frustrated. They will tell me their story.

Then I ask them, 'Boy, with everything you've been through, you still want to be here with us?'

This isn't something happens every day. But what I often hear is, 'Yeah, but you guys are so great, you're so nice.' They like the relationship.

We tried maybe a couple different times to set them up on ACH (Automated Clearing House) on their checking account. We can't seem to get it right. And they are frustrated.

But they know we are good people here. They feel we want a relationship with them.

We don't just say, 'Next. Member number? What do you want? Your balance is this much. Goodbye.'

Or say, 'Hey, go over to that technology and use that because it's more expensive to talk to us.'

We are in the people business at Affinity Plus. We do banking here, but really we're in the relationship business. We are in the business of people.

Banking is what we do. People is who we are.

When I think about how it boosts our business, it's referrals. People say all the time, 'Go to Affinity Plus.' They will say, 'Go there because of the people.'

They say, 'Go there because they treat you right.'"

THE FOUNDATION OF BUSINESS

David Cornell, Coach and Speaker

"Relationship building is foundational to building business. If you just go in and say to people, here's my product, here's my service, here's what I do, you're going to have some level of success.

But if you go in and find out something about them: Who they are. What they do. What drives them. And you begin to build a relationship. Because when you have a relationship you build trust.

If you don't take time to build relationships with those people that you hope to work with, you may have some level of success, but I don't think it'll last very long. And I don't think you're going to last very long."

PERSONAL INTEREST IN PEOPLE

Deb Brown, Client Retention Specialist

" I think it's always helpful. As far as how to do it, I think it's just taking a personal interest in people. You know, like I mentioned finding out about their dog, finding out about their family, finding out about their hobbies, and then using those things to make a connection with them.

Find out more

And then when you make a connection on those things, you're more likely to connect on business terms, as well.

They talk over and over again in marketing about having the 'know, like, and trust' factor. And that's how you get to the sale.

Well, relationship building is exactly that. You're getting to know somebody, and they're getting to know you. Then they find out they like you because you like them, and you're doing nice things for them and showing an interest in them.

And then they trust you because you took the time to care about them, care about their dog, their family, or their interests, whatever it is."

REFERRALS

Debbie Magnuson, Coach, Facilitator and Consultant

"Well, the most obvious example is referrals, right?

One doesn't make referrals to a professional that you don't have a relationship with or don't trust. And so clearly, the most obvious benefit to the organization is the ability to build strong relationships that stand the test of time is referrals.

And I'm glad to say that in my organization, we get lots of referrals, and we get lots of people who want to work with us because of word of mouth.

It's that whole raving fan thing. Once you have built that relationship and established strong trust, then people want to tell others about you. And that's gratifying from a financial standpoint, but I have to say, it's much more gratifying from a personal standpoint. It means the most to me.

The money's great, but the personal relationship is much more valuable."

RIGHT FIT

Elizabeth Hagen, Coach

"I don't like to be sold to the minute I meet someone. I want to get to know somebody.

And I think that's important because as coaches, we shouldn't just let anybody hire us. It should only be someone who is our right fit or perfect-fit client.

And you only find that out by talking to them and building a relationship. Now, sometimes you can find that out in 30 minutes and you're good to go.

Other times, they need to get some newsletters for a while, some phone calls, some emails; it takes longer."

DIFFERENT KINDS OF RELATIONSHIPS

John Palen, Consultant, Coach, and Entrepreneur

" **R**elationship building will lead to referrals. It will lead to a deeper, more intimate working relationship. Where it can hurt and sometimes it can, is there are people who can take too much time. They're needier or they require more time and attention.

Other people don't require much time and attention, so I think there's a trick to identifying and managing the different types of relationships that different types of clients need. From one client to the next, that can vary. The type of relationship they want or need can be different from one client to the next. So, I need a mix of clients."

CAN'T FAKE IT

Kit Welchin, Speaker and Trainer

"I think the key to business relationships is you have to have a genuine interest in what your client is doing, facing, fighting, and struggling with. And what the outcome or success they are seeking. It is kind of hard to fake genuine interest."

RECIPROCITY

Lynette Crane, Introvert Coach

"I wouldn't be in business without the nurturing relationships. The ones I have nurtured and, in turn, reciprocated. It can be as simple as they're bolstering up my sagging spirits at those times we all have or they may provide resources out of a clear blue sky that I didn't know I needed and suddenly I needed them and there they were. Connections, those are some just off the top of my head."

A REAL PERSON

Nicole Antoinette, Change Agent

"I mean I think that relationships are everything. I don't think that that's new. I think that things change with social media. There's different ways. There are different mediums to which we have relationships, but at the end of the day, people work with people that they like - period.

I think that keeping that front and center and remembering that everyone is a real person, especially now, the fact that so much is done virtually. I mean my entire business is virtual. It's easy to forget that it's a real person, real feeling, who's sitting at the other side of the computer, reading an email and commenting. I have found it to be really helpful in boosting business and also just living with integrity to remember that everyone is a real person. Everyone has feelings like I have. People are always doing the best that they can in any situation, even if their best moment isn't that great.

It's trying to put a humanizing piece on everything, which can definitely be difficult when you're selling virtual products that get purchased by hundreds of people. We need to remember that each of these people, they're a real person. I don't do very much one-on-one work. I do it very selectively, but most of the time I'm working, I'm either creating a product, an online product for our site, or I'm creating small groups. I do small group coaching.

So, it's because I don't have that one-on-one interaction as much, it's even more important for me to like really keep that front and center that even if I'm thinking about 100 people, 300 people, that each person is just one person and for me."

TWO PHASES WITH GRATITUDE

Nicole Antoinette, Change Agent

❝ I see relationships in business kind of in two phases. The first is the start of a relationship where you're bringing people into your world and maybe that's the first time they've gotten my email, for example. That's the perfect time to set the tone for what they can expect from their relationship with you.

And then the second phase is where you're improving your relationships over time and I think that obviously is going to help certain relationships more than others.

I work on improving the relationships by under-promising and over-delivering, by taking time to make people feel special and then more than anything, I express gratitude. I found that gratitude is pretty much the number-one relationship-building tool, going out of your way to send a 'thank you' note. Be sincere to tell people that their work matters, both in terms of clients and colleagues in the field.

That has really helped a lot for me."

RELATIONSHIP BUILDING WITH THE NEXT GENERATION

Steve Lear, Financial Services Company President

" I've built a lot of great relationships with clients. Now it's a matter of building some great relationships with support staff so that we can continue to serve the clients to help them reach all of their goals and to overcome challenges.

As a veteran of the financial service industry, I think there's a time when you have to make this mental shift to mentoring the next generation. The purpose is for your firm to have ability to provide sustainable services to clients and their families, and create leverage in the service you provide.

I'm going to continue to foster my relationships with my clients and ask for recommendations, but it's a responsibility, then, to start building that relationship with a next generation, recognizing it could take 10 years for it to mature so that the clients continue to receive the best service."

MEET THE NEEDS

Tom Downing, Realtor

❝ I have found that if I'm developing a relationship at an open house, I only have a very short time to meet somebody.

About 76% of the people that come through a house during an open house are not working with a broker and will eventually because they're actively looking. So that's the number-one opportunity for people to really meet somebody that they might want to work with.

If I don't make that relationship work instantly and read what that person wants and needs and react and utilize all of the different resources in the right way, I'll either turn them off by being too aggressive or not provide enough information and they walk away.

So, I think it's the most critical element that I could possibly imagine for the career I'm in now."

KEEPING WHAT YOU WORKED FOR

Vicki Turnquist, Bank President

"The business sticks if you have a relationship. If you don't have a relationship, you have a transaction that's going to move at a lower rate or a friend went to another bank.

It [the relationship] boosts business by keeping what you worked so hard for on your books."

GO. GO. GO. TO BELONG

C. J. Hayden, Coach and Trainer

"I first got started in business before the Internet existed. So back then, my choices for marketing myself were a lot more limited. I think that was actually a benefit because I couldn't put up a website. I couldn't send out emails. Nobody was on email. Nobody had websites.

And so instead, I had to really look at three different avenues for building a professional services practice. I said, 'Well, okay, I can advertise,' and I certainly tried a little of that early on.

'Or I can send out a bunch of letters and try placing cold calls.' And, well, okay I tried a little bit of that.

'Or I can get to know people, and as a result of getting to know people, I can build my business either because I personally met people who can become clients or because I get to know people who are referral sources for me.' And that was actually what I chose and where I started very, very early. I need to know more people.

I didn't have a wide enough network of people who could be my clients or people who can refer me to clients. So, I'm going to go to meetings, I'm going to attend seminars. I'm going to have coffee. And what that led to was other opportunities to give talks, write articles, other things that brought me clients.

But none of those opportunities would've materialized if I wasn't doing the other stuff. If I wasn't going to the meetings, if I wasn't having the coffee, if I wasn't taking steps to get to know people. So, it's really a very, very essential step, not just in the mechanics of building the business,but in really feeling as if I was a professional among peers.

If I belong in this world, instead of feeling as if I am excluded and out there knocking on doors, trying to get people to pay attention to me. Feeling like I belonged was really important to keep me going at the beginning."

FOCUS AND TOOLS

Dave Hubers, Financial Services Company past President

"The key is having advisors who are relationship focused and, secondly, giving them the tools they need, like financial planning software, to be able to do that. Because we sell more product and we retain the clients longer when we've done a

financial plan, assets grow faster. Thus, both of those help build business."

GETTING VALUE

Lisa Magnotta, Company President

"We've been in business for 24 years, and I have some clients that have been with us since almost the beginning. And what we've found with those folks is if there's someone else that comes along, a competitor trying to muscle in on my territory, so to speak, those clients will call us and say, 'You know, you need to come over and talk with us. We're getting this and we're getting this pitch. They're showing me prices.' And we can say, 'Well, here's what it is.'

And often times it either means we can educate the client on what the competitor is really trying to sell them or it may be to their benefit that we change our prices if someone's trying to undercut.

Relationships aren't always about getting the cheapest deal. We try to promote that we have value. We're not the cheapest out there, we're not the most expensive, but we want you to feel like it's a good value.

It's just like anything. I mean, you, as a consumer, you don't want to go out and buy the cheapest thing that you can. You don't buy the cheapest car. You don't buy the cheapest suit, but you don't want to pay more than you should.

So, we try to sell our services. A lot of that is once our clients have been with us and once we have that relationship, they see the value and that trust, and the integrity of our research is part of that value."

QUESTION 4

When you think about nurturing relationships in business, do you have an experience that you would like to share?

GIVE BACK

Ajay Mandal, IT Company President

" Honesty and performance are important. Here is an example from a referral that was over two years old.

I did a project of a couple of months and made decent money on that project. I made it a point to give back 10% of the money I made to the company that had referred me even though it was three years back.

Honesty is very important. And making sure there's some sort of pat on the back and financial commitment to the person who generated business for you."

TIME INVESTED

Alyssa Granlund, Marketing Consultant

"I guess some of the things I've found that have worked pretty well for me as far as nurturing relationships is that a lot of times when I look back over my clients, ones that I've been able to work with long-term, I tend to have given them quite a bit of time prior to ever being hired by them.

It might just be time talking about what it is that they need or brainstorming with them or just really kind of good faith showing what I can do and taking time to building relationships.

Eventually, they do usually end up hiring me out for whatever work it is and we've got a really firm foundation to work from.

But it does take that initial time and effort from me to kind of get to know them before we can move forward."

EXPONENTIAL RELATIONSHIPS

Amy Scott, Coach and Editor

"There is one person who comes to mind. I can't remember how I met him at the start. It is interesting to trace back how you got connected with somebody to begin with.

So, this is a guy who is a copywriter and so he writes for clients and then also had done some of his own writing. So, this is a contact for my editing business.

I believe we had an in-person mutual friend who mentioned my name when he said that he was looking for an editor. So, he got in touch with me. And this was probably three years ago.

And since then, he will check in occasionally and Skype and just say hi. We keep in touch. We worked on I think three projects together, two books of his and then a book that he hired me to help a client with.

And as time goes on, we get to know each other better. We get to know how the other person works. Now, he continues to refer other people to me when they say they are looking for an editor.

So, from one initial contact, it has turned into kind of an exponential relationships that have come out of that as well as work and revenue that has come out of that."

WHAT'S THE PASSION?

Harrison Nelson, Adviser

"You've got to figure out what their passion is. And that's how you can be a friend to them, through something they really care about."

STAYING IN TOUCH

Mac Gordon, Insurance Agent

"**W**hen I first started in the insurance business I was making cold calls. Many times I would hear, 'I'm not looking right now, but stay in touch with me.'

I would continue to follow up with them every six months or every year. And one guy in particular who I just spoke with again today who's been a client for 14 years.

Initially, he let me quote his insurance, but I was not competitive with his current carrier.

I continued follow-up with him with his permission and it was year in, year out. Eventually, he said you know Mac I haven't heard from my agent for five years and I've continued to hear from you.

We ended up working together. He owned the business so we wrote his business insurance. We also wrote his family insurance which included his two daughters his brother.

It's been one of those relationships that has grown into a friendship.

We continue to talk and to stay in touch."

SAY NO TO NURTURE RELATIONSHIPS

Nicole Antoinette, Change Agent

" I think that one of the most common things that I've experienced and that I found amongst entrepreneurs is that they feel overworked, stressed within and taken advantage of. There's this idea that you have to be working 14-hour days and just be hustling all the time.

I know that I felt that way for a long time. It's really something. When I build relationships in business, I think that I need to be everything to everyone and that we need to get every request. We need to answer every question. But once we do that, we're actually not doing what's best for each relationship, I found.

It's not success for us and it's not success for our relationships that we quickly find we're resenting the people that we went into business to serve in the first place. It's not their fault that we're overworked. It's our fault because we're not managing our time and our energy properly and that they kind of wind up paying the brunt factor and we get frustrated with clients or it shows in our work.

So, again when I think about nurturing relationships in business, one of the best relationship nurturing practices for me has been the art of gracefully saying no to things or hopefully gracefully saying no to things that aren't in line with my top priority. That actually lets you keep your focus on the people and the project that you are going to do and to really prioritize that.

I think that you teach people how to treat you and nurture relationships. In order to nurture relationships, I think you have to know what's not important in order to be able to nurture the relationships that are important."

OFFLINE ONLINE

Tena Pettis, Social Media Company Owner

"So, I really love offline relationships when I can really connect with someone face to face. Have coffee with them. Meet them at a networking event.

Show up at their business when I can connect with them and see what they do and what they are passionate about and what they love.

But what I've really found is that being able to take a relationship like that and then put it online, it sounds crazy, but I've been able to strengthen them.

 I have clients all over the United States, and if it wasn't for social media and it wasn't for email, I wouldn't be able to connect with them, like, ever. So that part has been really big for me, to create those relationships online, as well as, strengthen them there. To be able to connect them with people who are already in my CLIQ or my circle."

THEY CAN TELL WHEN YOU CARE

Tom Downing, Realtor

"I'll just pick the most recent one that comes to mind. As I mentioned, I'm new to the area. I spoke with a woman who came into my open house. She was sort of interested in that house but not really.

Just by asking her really simple questions that really were the questions that I know are most important to her, we were able to develop a relationship very, very quickly. By the end of our 45-minute conversation, she had called up and fired her other agent.

We ended up buying a house the next week together, which we closed on February 14. It was my first sale. If I hadn't really stopped and listened to her….

I think people can tell when you care. There's no gimmicks to any of this. I think it's actually a sincerity that comes across, both for a business and for an individual that people pick up on right away."

INVESTING IN START UPS

Chuck Palmer, Financial Services Regional Managing Director

"We've been quite active with emerging businesses, with Angel Network, with Life Science Alley, with The Collaborative, and with other organizations.

Through those relationships, we then would connect with a business that really needed a firm our size with the capabilities we have. They needed the help that we can offer. But, frankly, they were with a very small financial services firm because what they can afford today was to get their bookkeeping done or to maybe get a review of some kind done.

We're willing to go in selectively, wisely, and build a relationship with them by investing time and resources with them that we understand we may not get paid for. Or we may get paid a heavily discounted rate until they become a much larger organization. So we've invested both our time and our resources, whatever they might be. It might be IT resources. It might be human resource consulting. It might be, you know, some other types of work: advising them on their personal taxes, that kind of thing. We're willing to make those kinds of investments to build a long-term relationship with that client."

FOLLOW ADVICE

Theresa Rose, Speaker, Author, Mentor

" Following advice is one of the things that is so important about building relationships in business.

Everyone has their own levels of expertise and areas of expertise; so, when a true relationship is built and someone suggests to do A, B, or C.

Do A, B, or C. Follow through. That is one of the keys of really growing a relationship is when someone takes a times to sit with you and says, 'Here is what I recommend you can do to further your career.'

Do it because they know what they're doing. Even if they don't know what they're doing, you've shown that you respect them enough to try to do what they said to do.

And trust that they are out for your best interest and that doors will open as a result of it.

Often times we get advice from people. We have 'sit downs' in relationships and networking. And then we don't follow-up. We don't do what they said. But when we do unbelievable doors open.

Because then they see, 'Oh, she heard me.' And they'll do it again. And they'll do it again. And they'll do it again.

That's the key to the cultivating relationships part, actually follow-through with the advice and suggestions and the connections that are made."

BUILDING THE RELATIONSHIP

Deirdre Van Nest, Professional Speaker, Coach

"Well, I have one client who is probably one of my best clients. What I mean by that is he has done every single thing I've offered. Everything.

We were introduced through a mutual business acquaintance. The first thing he was interested in having me do was come in for a speaking engagement.

I probably had three-hour-long conversations with him before he hired me, on the phone. And I thought by the third conversation when he called again, 'This guy is never going to hire me.'

I thought, 'What is taking this guy so long to make a decision?' He did make the decision on the third call.

And since then, he's a raving fan. He takes everything I've offered. I offer. He does it.

He's a real analytical type and he needed to have all the ducks in a row. He had to have the decision points. And he had to have a sense of me.

I was thinking, 'Why am I talking to this guy again?'

But if I hadn't, look what wouldn't have happened. And I really enjoy him. I've been able to really help them. And I've been able to see him grow.It's been a very enjoyable business relationship.

P.S.: Seven months later: A few months ago, he recommended me for a speaking engagement. So far, that one talk has brought in more than $40,000 of income."

QUESTION 5

If you could say one thing to the readers of this book with regards to strengthening relationships, what would it be?

BE YOURSELF

Allen Vaysberg, IT Entrepreneur

"Be yourself. Be authentic, be genuine, and understand that relationships in business are no different from relationships in personal life.

You are who you are, and people will either like you or not. It doesn't matter what you sell. It doesn't matter what you do. If they like you, they will deal with you. Otherwise, they will not."

DO WHAT YOU SAY

Barbara Sanderson, Coach

❝ I think, 'Do what you say you're going to do. And if for some reason you can't, immediately contact the person and renegotiate.'"

LESS IS MORE FOR IMPACT

Buffie Blesi, Coach

❝ Less is more is going to be my thing. What I mean by that: less individuals, less people, deeper relationships.

Don't just scratch the surface. I can go back early in my business and think about people. I have database of these people. They are on my newsletter list. I see their name and recognize the name and I might even recognize the time I met them but I have no relationship with them anymore. I might even have met them for coffee or lunch or something.

When I look back and I think, 'What could I have really done better there?' I would've been more selective. And then the people that I did select to really not just meet for a nice time, but I would ask, 'Now what? What's next for us? Where do we go with this relationship?'

And I still don't always do it, but every time I do, I find that it's enduring. It's profitable for them or for me or both. I leave feeling good about it.

So, the less is more thing is there. You don't have to be everything all people. What you need to do is you need to find the right connection and the right person to be able to make some kind of impact. And for me it's always about impact. I need to be relevant in somebody's life in my business and everything else at the end of the day."

IT'S NOT HARD

C. J. Hayden, Coach and Trainer

"It doesn't have to be that hard.

It's something that we as humans very, very naturally do. I mean, our lives in our very first moments on this planet are built around relationships. And I think we just have to allow ourselves to be authentically human in the business world with the people who we want and need to be interacting with to achieve our career and business goals.

I feel as if where we get tripped up is that we try and layer technique on it and attach all of this artificiality to it. We feel like we need to be, I don't know, some mythical salesperson who we imagine, who has everybody's wives' and husbands' and children's birthdays in a calendar and is mechanically calling them up to wish the not very

sincere greetings on occasions that don't matter to the person who's placing the calls. You know?

No, that's not what it's about. It's about enjoying the company of and liking the people who you interact with in business enough so that you want to spend time with them. You're enjoying being with them. You're liking going to coffee and having phone conversations.

If you're not, how could you possibly build relationships? And I think that's what people need to recognize. It's got to be authentic.

It's got to be real. It's not just a whole bunch of techniques you can learn and then try to apply without any heart behind it."

GOLDEN RULE

Chuck Palmer, Financial Services Regional Managing Director

"Well, you said these are top of mind answers. What comes to my mind is the golden rule still applies.

If you treat people like you want to be treated, you will always gain in the long run."

CREATE A CULTURE

Dave Hubers, Financial Services Company past President

"It would be creating a culture in the organization, both in the home office and in the field that values relationships and knows how to build them and retain them.

I do believe you've got to create the right environment to make that happen.

Companies have different strengths or niches. You have companies that are very strong on building transaction volume. You have companies who are very strong on operations.

You have companies who are very strong at building relationships. All those require different skills tools sets and different cultures.

If you're going to be in the relationship building business, you've got to have the culture, the environment that is conducive to that and you have to attract people who can empathize with the customer. You need to understand the customer and be able to relate to them."

DON'T STOP WORKING IT

Dave Larson, Credit Union President

"You have to do it. You have to strengthen relationships.

You have to strengthen relationships whether it's kids, marriage, or business.

Every time I've seen a relationship fail, every time a relationship of mine has failed, what happened? Someone stopped working at it.

Why do they fail? The communication stops. The effort stops around the relationship. That's when people get strange and things fall apart."

BUILD LAYERS

David Cornell, Coach and Speaker

"I think relationships have layers. And I think the more you can do to layer that relationship the more you strengthen it.

And then when you have challenges in the business if you have a really thick layer at your foundation you'll be able to work through those things."

FASTER THAN ADVERTISING

Deb Brown, Client Retention Specialist

"The key to growing your business is to have great client retention and referrals, and the key to all of that is your relationships.

That will grow a business faster than any advertising that you can do. The relationships and then that just naturally leads to client retention and more referrals."

BE INTENTIONAL

Debbie Magnuson, Coach, Facilitator, and Consultant

"Be intentional about building relationships. Don't think that it's just going to happen.

I think that leaders need to be thoughtful and strategic. I mean, it sounds kind of cold to say, 'Be strategic about relationships,' but it's like anything else. The things we plan for are much more likely to happen.

I think we need to be thoughtful and compassionate, and I also think we need to be planful and intentional about our actions. Simple stuff like reach out to five people this week. Stay in touch, be a friend, especially, when it comes to networking. Be available because there's one thing as a career coach I've learned very strongly: 'You never know when you're going to be the one needing a career network.'

So, I think leaders inside organization need to be much more thoughtful and intentional about that."

FOCUS ON SERVICE

Deirdre Van Nest, Professional Speaker, Coach

❝I believe making sure that I focus on service to the client first and that what we do together is a good fit is a great basis for relationships."

DON'T THINK OF YOURSELF

Elizabeth Hagan, Coach and Consultant

❝To not think about yourself. What does that person that you meet need for their business for their life? Think in terms of them not think terms of what you want. What do they need?"

BE A FRIEND

Harrison Nelson, Coach and Consultant

"I think simply to be a friend. Act towards this person as you would act towards any friend, any true friend. Always look for opportunities where you can be the first person to help them before

you ask them to help you because whatever your product is they are going to help you by buying your product.

And sometimes they are going to pay you more for that product than they could for some competitor's product. You can befriend them to start to with."

GOLDEN RULE

James Olsen, Attorney

"Treating others and treating the relationship how you want them to treat you: the Golden Rule.

Remembering it takes effort. It is one of the things you just have to start doing. It's interesting to see where it goes."

IT'S THE LITTLE THINGS

Jenny Foss, Job Search Strategist

"I think a big part of the message is it's the little things that can make a huge, huge difference. Like I mentioned a few minutes ago, making it loud and clear through everything that you do that there's a big 'we care' factor running through you as an individual and whatever business you represent. I mean, it just can be so huge.

We live and work in a culture that everyone is moving 90 million miles an hour. There is just so much automated this, transactional that. If you can as a professional be the one that demonstrates continually in any small ways this 'we care' factor, it will be noted because, frankly, it's not that common, I don't think, anymore. And so, coming out as a genuine, helpful, caring individual who is out for the best interest of the people that you serve, I think it's just the winning formula."

BE MINDFUL OF THE OTHER PERSON

John Palen, Consultant, Coach, and Entrepreneur

"Be authentic and mindful of what the other person in the relationship wants and needs."

BE SINCERE

....

Lisa Magnotta, Company President

....

"I think you need to be sincere, that's the thing.

A client relationship, even though you're not out to be everybody's friend because you still need to have some sort of boundary there, still needs to be sincere and you still need to truly express your appreciation for their business.

Whatever service you're providing them has to be your best, each and every order, whether it's cleaning their house, whether it's providing them an abstract, whether it's selling them a widget.

Every contact you have with that client is another opportunity to solidify that relationship, and so, I think truly being sincere, truly having the integrity so that what you're giving them each and every time is the best that you can at the moment.

And being willing, also, if something goes wrong, to stand behind that. Nothing really proves your service to your client better than how you perform when there's a mistake made, when there's a disappointment that happens. You basically apologize for it and you obviously credit the client for whatever that costs.

You do it again, and then you go back and you figure out what happened so it doesn't happen again. And you convey that all to the client with, 'We're sorry this happened. We're sorry this was an inconvenience. We're sorry we disappointed you. Here's what happened. We're going to make sure we're taking steps so it doesn't happen again.'

And make sure it doesn't happen again, that's truly the test of a vendor.

What happens when they do disappoint you? We've had it happen to us. We've had vendors that we gone after and said, 'This was wrong.' And they were like, 'Well, whatever.' I don't use them again. When they don't make it right.... You have to try and make it right."

APPRECIATION

Lynette Crane, Introvert Coach

"**G**et out of judgment and into appreciation of others."

BE CONSISTENT

Mac Gordon, Insurance Agent

"**C**onsistency.

Find ways to stay in front of people to find out what they need and remind them what you're doing."

HAVE FUN

Mark Santi, Business Attorney and Litigator

"**B**e Genuine. Have fun.

Networking can be unpleasant if you want to look at it that way. And folks can sense you are doing a task rather than being a human being. If you have to network, why not have fun? Why not build a friendship while doing it? Why not take it as an opportunity to learn?

One of the best ways to network is to show a genuine interest in someone else and thereby learn from them. People love to share what they know with you. So, listening is a much better tool than talking when it comes to networking.

By listening, you learn and you do a favor to the person talking. And I think that favor will be returned with a genuine affection for you.

And hopefully, that will lead to a healthy relationship with that person and potentially business in the future."

HONOR CLIENTS

Mary Ann Heine, Bank Officer

" I think that I'm able to do it because I'm confident in myself. I have experience. I've seen a lot and I honor my clients. I very much respect them. I don't look at them as dollar signs. I look at them as people with interesting backgrounds that have been able to amass some wealth and some income, and that's always interesting. So I really, really like people and honor them and I've come through."

HONESTY

Michael Lane, Company President

" Honesty. I think for the relationships to be effective there has to a certain amount of honesty that's underlying everything that's there. There has to be total honesty."

KEY TO SUCCESS

Mike Reis, IT Consultant

"The key to success is building relationships."

GOAL

Scott Plum, Sales Trainer

"What is the goal? Converting relationships to revenue we need to know what the goal is.

There are hunters and there are farmers when it comes to relationships. Sales people need to have a relationship as a hunter to convert it to a client.

Farmers need to have that relationship as an account manager to maintain and keep it and keep the competition out."

BE AUTHENTIC

Sonia Fortier, Marketing Consultant

"You should be genuine and authentic. Just touch base. No selling. By your behavior and actions saying, 'I know you. I like you. I'm touching base.'"

RELATIONSHIP NURTURING IS NOT NETWORKING

Stephanie Laitala-Rupp, Owner of Bookkeeping and CFO Service

"One of the things that we have learned is, there is a difference between networking and relationship nurturing. Networking can bleed you dry on every level. It's exhausting if you do it. It's really exhausting. The relationship nurturing is sort of the antithesis of that.

The trick comes in understanding how often you need to network to start developing a relationship and then how do you transition from networking to nurturing and who do you transition with because you're not going to have relationships with every single solitary person you meet. It just is impossible.

And it will allow you to focus once you identify who are people that give you energy and who are people that you have the synergy with because of the shared goals or the shared values or the shared interests and let go of those that aren't, that aren't those things.

It becomes much more rewarding because you can focus your time on the things that add value instead of nickel-and-dimeing your time with those that don't."

MAKE IT A PRIORITY

Steve Callender, Coach and Trainer

"To always make it a priority. It's one of those things that sometimes when you get busy on project work or busy on other things, you may let go.

It's one thing that you have to have the discipline to maintain, and I would actually advocate for setting it up as a task on your calendar or on your to-do list so that at a certain point on each month or each fortnight, you give yourself a reminder. 'Call Joe' or 'touch base with Michael' or something like that. You know, just so that you don't let that slip because it really is one of the most important things you can do."

IT TAKES TIME

Steve Lear, Financial Services Company President

"Time. It will take time and it's very rewarding."

BE AUTHENTIC

Steve Wilcox, Coach and Consultant

"Authentic. I think one has to be genuine and authentic. I think you cannot mask, in any relationship, an aspect of who you are and what you stand for. You need to be straight up.

Not always will that individual embrace who you are and what you stand for, but you have to be authentic in your representation. And those that embrace that authenticity and the facts about who you are and what they stand for, they'll become lifelong friends and lifelong relationships. I think that's the most critical part.

We're not put on this earth for very long. I think you collect [relationships] carefully and protect constantly."

BE GENUINE

Tena Pettis, Social Media Company Owner

"It has to be genuine. I myself am a connector, and I love relationships. But if I didn't, it wouldn't come off as authentic or genuine, and people would see right through that. So, I'd say surrounding yourself with people that you genuinely can get excited about and about their business and what they do. Creating relationships with people like that is key.

But it really, truly has to be genuine, and you really have to really, truly care about that person."

GET OUT OF YOUR OWN HEAD

Teresa Thomas, Director of Woman's Networking Organization

"When it comes to strengthening relationships, I think the key thing is to get out of your own head and think about how you can be helpful, how you can be a resource.

It does several things. It increases your confidence because you're not so worried how you're coming across. You're developing your reputation for what you have to offer, what you know, and what you're able to provide. I do feel like that's the key thing: thinking big picture and getting outside of your own head to develop quality ongoing relationships."

BE SERVICE ORIENTED

Theresa Rose, Speaker, Author, Mentor

"Always act from a service oriented approach. How can you help the other person? That is how you do it. If you operate from a heart centered service oriented perspective in each and every connection you have, doors open that you couldn't possibly have expected to open."

ONLY ENDURING THING

Tim Brands, IT Company President

"Regardless of the type of people, the type of business, personally, professionally, spiritually, I mean, really the only thing that we have enduring is relationships. They take a lot of work, and in the end, we have to make a choice. We have to make decisions every day on whether we are going to invest in and nurture the relationships of those people who are closest and most important to us or we're going to choose not to."

BE PASSIONATE ABOUT IT

Tom Downing, Realtor

"If you are not passionate about it or if you are not willing to at least entertain passion as part of your approach to this, then you probably really should consider doing something else because I just don't think you can fake that kind of thing. I think it has to be something that you really believe and can demonstrate."

TOO MUCH TOO LITTLE

Tom Laughlin, Executive Coach

"If you're worried that you're not doing relationship building, you're probably doing too much. If you're not worried that you are doing it, you're probably not doing enough."

GIVERS GAIN

Tom Majewski, Video and Marketing Consultant

"I may have been to one too many BNI meetings but the first thing that pops into my mind is 'givers gain.'

As much as I use my network and the relationships I've formed to seek business I also am as active as possible in listening to what that network and reaching out to people that I think I can help or make the connection for.

Whenever I have a coffee with someone or catch up, I'm very adamant, as we're leaving I try to say, 'If there's anything I can help with a connection that I can make please let me know.'

As important as it is to use a network to your advantage, it is also important to help people build relationships."

BE HUMBLE

Tom O'Neill, Company President

"You know, I'd think I say to study what it means to be humble. I think that if you did, you'd find out that people that are humble, it doesn't mean they're meek, it doesn't mean they're not confident, it doesn't mean they're weak.

It means that they seek first to understand. It means that they ask questions. It means that they truly want to know and to empathize with the people that they're trying to build a relationship with."

DON'T TAKE THEM FOR GRANTED

Vicki Turnquist, Bank President

"Don't take them [the relationships] for granted. Just because you had it [a relationship] a year ago, you have to keep building on it."

THINK STRATEGIC WITH HEART

Wendy Blomseth, Photographer and Marketer

"Two opposite things. I can never do one. One is think strategic. What is your timeline? What is your budget? How much are you going to invest?

And then also come from a place of genuine heart, trustworthy, love, caring, kindness, and gratitude.

It's walking both the left brain/ right brain, heart, and business."

Scan this code or visit
www.thebookonfollowup.com/interviewees
to know more about the interviewees.

Planning->Systems->Follow-up->Results

Has something you've read so far resonated with you? Something to cause you to think, "Hmm, we need to look at some part of our client acquisition and retention system?" Or, "I want to work on something to help our sales team be more effective in follow-up so that they build better relationships and trust with customers and prospects for themselves and the company."

If the answer is "No", then thank you for reading the book. Please pass it on to someone else.

If the answer is "Yes", then read on to go deeper.

A purpose of Section 1 is to illustrate "No follow-up, no consistent results."

The idea behind Systems for Strengthening Relationships™ (Systems) is that you must have systems for consistent follow-up.

No systems, no consistent follow-up.

The systems are built of three major concepts:

- Know who your customers are, so that, you can duplicate the ones you can be most effective helping and who best fit your company, culture and product.
- Know what to say to them and when, so that, you can create and nurture relationships and trust.
- Know how the sales team will consistently maintain follow-up with your prospects and customers, so that, your sales professionals will create and nurture relationships and trust with customers and prospects.

The next five chapters cover these three areas and the planning needed.

This is neither rocket science, nor is it difficult, but it does require planning.

No planning, no systems.

Section 3 will discuss where planning for Systems for Strengthening Relationships™ fits in the larger planning process.

SYSTEMS FOR STRENGTHENING RELATIONSHIPS™

WHAT ARE SYSTEMS?

Systems for Strengthening Relationships™ (Systems) is both a way of nurturing relationships and trust with customers and prospects; as well as, a way of assuring that sales professionals follow-up with customers and prospects in a consistent manner that is compatible with organizational goals, vision, mission, results, culture, etc.

Systems organize your thinking and actions so that sales professionals effectively create and nurture mutually-beneficial relationships with customers and prospects in order to boost business.

WHY DO I NEED SYSTEMS?

If you do not currently have something similar to Systems for Strengthening Relationships™ (Systems), you are losing customers and prospects from your sales process. Some studies show that as high as 48% of sales professionals do not make a second contact with prospects. Systems help those sales professionals create and nurture the relationships and trusts that will be mutually beneficial.

HOW DO I CREATE SYSTEMS?

You create Systems for Strengthening Relationships™ first in the planning process then in the implementation. The creation and maintenance of systems need to be included in the strategic plan, the operational business plan and as a project plan.

SEGMENTING CUSTOMERS

WHAT?

Segmenting is identifying the characteristics of the people you can best serve. This in a sales context would start with those who would benefit from the product or service most or who have the biggest problem that the product or service will solve.

The information available on the Internet about segmenting is extensive. For that reason, I am not going to include any more information on what it is. Please search "segmenting customers" on the Internet.

I have my approach to segmenting and you should find the approach that you are most comfortable with. To go deeper into this and hear about my approach to segmenting, contact me for a complementary Initial Strategy Session.

WHY?

It allows you to focus your communication and interactions with customers in a way that is most likely to be mutually beneficial. It allows you to be able to be more specific and intentional in your communications and interactions.

HOW?

A simple approach is to identify three categories and labels. An example would be "best" client, "okay" client and "so-so" client.

You then go through your client list using whichever criteria you have decided upon, and put the client into one of the three categories. After you've done that, you look at the clients in each category to make sure that there is a sense of similarity and that that similarity matches your original criteria.

This allows you to identify your best clients.

You want all the "best" clients you can find. You should believe that "okay" clients have the possibility of becoming "best" clients. The "so-so" clients you have little or no expectation of but you haven't fired them yet.

Then you accumulate as many behaviors and other indicators for each type of client. First, this information will allow you to more effectively nurture the relationship and trust with this client. In addition, it helps you, when you meet a prospective customer to identify which segment they may fall into as a customer.

This is how segmenting benefits the sales process, as well as customer retention.

Email: michael@cavittassociates.com
Phone: 612-216-4859
Skype: jmichael.cavitt

Screen Tip: Please send me an email or call me to discuss a complementary Session.

CREATING CAMPAIGNS

WHAT?

Campaigns are a series of actions taken by individuals or initiated by software. The actions are selected from the media menu.

Campaigns are also composed of a series of decisions implemented by sales professionals. The decisions concern the actions which will encourage a customer to deepen the relationship with the company and become an advocate. The initial planning looks first at the Customer Tier and the segments in the Systems for Strengthening Relationships™ model and then at the other Tiers of the model but the core planning of campaigns needs to be with the customers.

There is a line of thinking that argues that campaigns for customers are not part of sales but are part of customer service.

While customer service campaigns are certainly important, sales campaigns should not overlook existing customers because they will make additional purchases, give referrals and can become advocates.

WHY?

The benefit of a campaign is to support a sales professional with a series of actions which assist him or her to nurture a relationship and trust with a customer or prospect at a level appropriate for the mutual benefit of the client or prospect and the company.

It also captures for the company the relationship with the customer or prospect so that when the sales professional leaves, the company is able to maintain that asset.

HOW?

The follow-up campaign answers three questions: Who, What, and How.

You create a campaign by:

- Crafting a message: the What,
- Selecting an appropriate medium: the How, and
- Communicating the message to an individual: the Who.

The Who is the person you want to follow-up with to nurture a relationship and build trust so that they will move through the steps connecting the Tiers.

The ultimate purpose is to nurture your "best" prospects to become advocates. Along the way a relationship and trust will develop with mutual benefit.

MAINTAINING CONSISTENT FOLLOW-UP

WHAT?

Sales professionals should maintain consistent follow-up using the campaigns created so that relationships are created and nurtured and trust is built to the mutual benefit of the organization, staff and the customers.

Consistency of follow-up means having staff, real or virtual, or electronic support for the sales professionals which assures that the campaigns will be carried out.

Consistency means the sales staff maintains the campaigns that are created using the support supplied by the organization.

Consistency of follow-up for Systems for Strengthening Relations™ means the sales staff regularly uses the campaigns in a manner that fits their Kolbe MO™.

Consistency of follow-up means prospects and customers are reached by the campaigns; so that, they have stronger relationships and trust with the brand and the people in the organization.

WHY?

First, the buyer/user of the product or service benefits from receiving the information, expressions of gratitude, recognition of their importance, etc.

Second, the sales staff benefits from helping prospects and customers build the relationship with them, the brand and their company. Some of the benefits of consistent follow-up are stronger relationships, more referrals, and more sales.

HOW?

Consistent follow-up is maintained when sales professionals or support staff take the action defined in the campaign. You need to identify sales professionals who can maintain the campaigns on their own and those that require support staff. Provide the support staff to those that need it and offer it to those that don't. Support staff can be real or virtual. You add an action step to the strategic plan and the operational business plan to create or upgrade support for sales professionals so that they effectively use Systems for Strengthening Relationships™ (Systems). Create a project plan to create Systems including evaluation. Execute the project plan. Review execution. Modify the systems.

MEDIA OF COMMUNICATION

WHAT?

Marshall McLuhan said, "The medium is the message." How [the medium] people receive a concept or information from you affects the concept or information they receive. So, the media is a separate chapter to emphasize this even though the choice of media is part of the campaign planning.

A communication is a concept transmitted by a medium.

When you send a thank you note, the choice of medium— handwritten note, typed note, Internet-based postal note, email, text message, any of the evaporating message services, etc.—all have a subtly different impact on the reader and their relationship to the concept, thank you, you sent.

WHY?

Marshall McLuhan said, "The medium is the message." While in business it is not as critical as in the media and entertainment industries, it is important to consider which medium is being used for which person or generational group.

Concepts are perceived differently by generational groups depending on the medium used.

HOW?

When the team is planning the project of Systems for Strengthening Relationships™, they should make up a Media Menu. A Media Menu is a list of media which are complementary and effective with your customers, your brand, your culture, and your product. If you are to gain a comprehensive knowledge of the media, you will need to do some research. The short list of media is verbal, [spoken, and written words] and nonverbal [actions, or behaviors, rather than words].

Scan this code or visit
www.thebookonfollowup.com/initial-strategy-session
to get more information about the Initial Strategy Session.

SECTION 3

The Order of Business™

The Order of Business™ is a model applied here to creating Systems for Strengthening Relationships™.

The Order of Business™

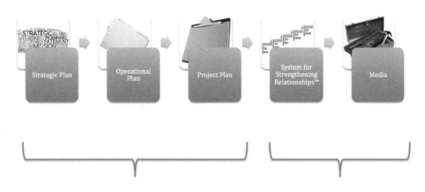

THE ORDER OF BUSINESS™

THE MODEL

The Order of Business™ model consists of five parts. The key module for us is The System for Strengthening Relationships™ (System). The System is the fourth module of the model. It is the pivotal part of the model in this case.

When you have an effective System, consistently applied, you are able to easily, conveniently create and develop relationships to have an effective network for gathering and keeping customers and clients.

The Model consists of five modules. Reading from left to right the parts are Strategic Planning, Operational Planning, Project Plan, System, and Media.

The next module to the left of the System is the Project Plan. When the System is created in a Project Plan for effective marketing or sales, it increases the effectiveness of the System.

The module to the left of the Project Plan is an Operational Plan. When the Project Plan is a strategy in an Operational Plan it increases the effectiveness of the system even more.

The last module to the left is the Strategic Plan. When an organization or company is large enough to engage in strategic planning, having the Operational Plan be a derivative of the Strategic Plan increases the effectiveness of the system.

The module to the right of Systems is Media. The basic categories of media are verbal [spoken and written words], and nonverbal [actions or behaviors rather than words]. A critical consideration in selection of media is Marshall McLuhan's quote, "The medium is the message."

12

SYSTEMS FOR STRENGTHENING RELATIONSHIPS™

Systems for Strengthening Relationships™

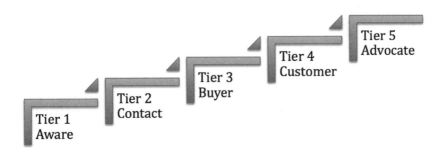

Tier 1
Aware

Tier 2
Contact

Tier 3
Buyer

Tier 4
Customer

Tier 5
Advocate

THE SYSTEM

The System for Strengthening Relationships™ (System) is a five-tier stair step.

People are broken down into these five categories:

- **Tier 1. Aware.** These are the people you are aware of. People with whom you have had no contact but you think might be someone who can move to a contact.
- **Tier 2. Contact.** This tier represents people with whom you've had contact. The contact can be face-to-face or through email or telephone.
- **Tier 3. Buyer.** These are the people who have done business with you one time. These are your most valuable resource.
- **Tier 4. Customer.** This tier represents people who have done business with you or your company more than once.
- **Tier 5. Advocate.** There is a small percentage of your Customers who when presented with a problem by someone, a problem you can solve, says, "Call John because he can solve your problem." These are your raving fans. Take good care of them.

The planning that we covered in Chapters 6 through 10 is about moving people from tier to tier.

You follow these steps:

1. You take the people who are in your Customer Tier and segment them.
2. You created a Media Menu and use it to create campaigns to help people move up the tiers. Campaigns are grouped into Systems.
3. You determine how to help your sales force use the campaigns consistently so that they are effective.

The planning of systems covered in Chapters 6 through 10 should also consider three conditions: People who camp out on a step, those who leave the system, and those who are willing to move up.

Scan this code or visit
www.thebookonfollowup.com/boost-your-business-workshop
to know more how to Boost your Business Workshop.

AFTERWORD

NOW WHAT?

What will you do next now that you have finished the book?

It would seems to me you have three choices:

1. Ignore all that you read because you don't have a problem.
2. Use the information that you've learned in this book and start working on the problem of improving your systems for creating and nurturing relationships in order to boost your business. Congratulations! Just let me know if I can help.
3. You realize you have a problem or may have a problem but aren't sure how to proceed. Contact me for a complementary Initial Strategy Session.

I am an intuitive problem solver and a change agent. I help individuals and organizations solve problems and take advantage of opportunities. Through the concepts in this book I will help individuals and organizations solve the problem of ineffectiveness in sales staff and lost revenue.

J. Michael Cavitt
Cavitt Associates
Email: Michael@cavittassociates.com
Phone: 612-216-4859
Skype: jmichael.cavitt

APPENDIX

SHOCKING SALES STATISTICS AS IT RELATES TO FOLLOW UP

February 21, 2011
As posted on: www.followupsuccess.com

Truly shocking sales statistics as it relates to your follow up process:

48% of sales people never follow up with a prospect.
25% of sales people make a second contact and stop.
12% of sales people make more than three contacts.
02% of sales are made on the first contact.
03% of sales are made on the second contact.
05% of sales are made on the third contact.
10% of sales are made on the fourth contact.
80% of sales are made on the fifth to twelfth contact.

Creating and using a follow up system is a guaranteed way to grow your business. In fact with less than 52% of all sales people following up with their prospects you will not only grow your business but you will stand out amongst your peers.

And remember 80% of sales are made in the fifth to twelfth contact if you are in a market with heavy competition you literally eliminate your competitors by simply following up.

As posted on: www.followupsuccess.com

INTERVIEWEES

The following people contributed to this book first by being willing to be interviewed as part of my research; and secondly by contributing to my thinking about what this book should be.

For both these reasons, I am eternally grateful to them singularly and as a group. If you find the excerpt from the interview that I used in the book interesting, helpful, provocative, or anything else positive, please send a note to that person. It is a small token of reward for their sharing their insights. You can see complete contact information and a description of their business at www.thebookonfollowup/interviewees.

NICOLE ANTOINETTE
Owner
Life Less Bullshit
nicole@lifelessbullshit.com

BUFFIEBLESI
Owner
Workaround
buffie@workaroundtc.com

WENDY BLOMSETH
Audience Development
Minneapolis St Paul Business Journal
wblomseth@bizjournals.com

TIM BRANDS
President
iBusiness Solutions
tbrands@ibusiness-solutions.com

DEB BROWN
Client Retention Specialist
Touch Your Clients Heart
info@TouchYourClientsHeart.com

STEVE CALLENDER
President
Effective Learning For Growth
steve@effectivelearningforgrowth.com

DAVID CORNELL
President
Cultivate Courage
dave@cultivatecourage.com

LYNETTE CRANE
Women Heart Champion
Creative Life Changes
Lynette@CreativeLifeChanges.com

SUSIE DIRCKS
COO
Jeane Thorne
skd@jeanethorne.com

TOM DOWNING
Realtor
Edina Realty
TomDowning@edinarealty.com

SONIA FORTIER
Owner
S. F. Marketing
slfortier@sfmarketing.biz

JENNY FOSS
Coach
JobJenny.com LLC
jenny@jobjenny.com

MAC GORDON
Insurance Agent
Ray Smith Insurance Agency
mac@raysmithins.com

ALYSSA GRANLUND
Owner
Connexecute
alyssa@connexecute.com

ELIZABETH HAGAN
Owner
Elizabeth Hagen Enterprises, LLC
Elizabeth@ElizabethHagen.com

C. J. HAYDEN
Principal
Wings for Business LLC
cjh@cjhayden.com

MARY ANN HEINE
SVP Private Banking Manager
Minnesota Bank & Trust
mheine@mnbankandtrust.com

DAVE HUBERS
Ameriprise Financial
david.r.hubers@gmail.com

STEPHANIE LAITALA-RUPP
President
OWL Bookkeeping
stephanie@OwlBookkeepingAndCFO.com

MICHAEL LANE
President
Lofton Label
MLane@loftonlabel.com

DAVE LARSON
President
Affinity Plus Federal Credit Union
DLarson@affinityplus.org

MARK LARSON
Vice President
Waytek
mlarson@waytekwire.com

TOM LAUGHLIN
Leadership and
Management Instructor
CaravelaInc
tom@caravela.us

STEVE LEAR
President
Affiance Financial LLC
stevelear@affiancefinancial.com

LISA MAGNOTTA
President/CFO
Minnesota Abstract & Title Company
lisa@mnabstracttitle.com

DEBBIE MAGNUSON
Vice President Of Talent
Management
Career Partners International
Twin Cities
debra.magnuson@cpitwincities.com

TOM MAJEWSKI
Owner
Majewski Marketing And Media
tom@majewskimarketing.com

AJAY MANDAL
President
Intellixion
ajay.mandal@intellixion.com

HARRISON NELSON
Adviser
Harrison Nelson
harrison.nelson@comcast.net

MATT NYE
Insurance Agent
Farmers Insurance Group
mnye@farmersagent.com

TOM O'NEILL
President
The Nerdery
toneill@nerdery.com

JAMES OLSEN
Managing Partner
Morbey& Olsen, PLLP
james@morbeylaw.com

JOHN PALEN
Founder & CEO
Palen Enterprises, Inc.
jppalen@alliedexecutives.com

CHUCK PALMER
Regional Managing Director,
Midwest Region
Wipfli
cpalmer@wipfli.com

TENA PETTIS
Owner
Tenacious
tena@tenaciousedge.com

SCOTT PLUM
Negotiation Instructor
Minneasota Sales Institute
scott.plum@mnsales.com

MIKE REIS
Owner
The Nerd School
mike@nerdschool.com

THERESA ROSE
Inspirational Speaker
Theresa Rose
theresa@theresarose.com

BARBARA SANDERSON
Owner
Barbara Sanderson
barbaraesanderson@comcast.net

MARK SANTI
Partner
Thompson Hall SantiCerny& Dooley
msanti@thompsonhall.com

AMY SCOTT
Coach and Editor
Nomadtopia
amy@nomadtopia.com

CRYSTAL THIES
LinkedIn Ninja
crystal@crystalclearbuzz.com

TERESA THOMAS
Director
Women In Networking
director@mnwin.com

VICKI TURNQUIST
Chief Executive Officer,
President and Founder
Private Bank Minnesota
VickiT@pbmn.com

DEIRDRE VAN NEST
Professional Speaker and
Business Performance Coach
Accelerate Performance, LLC
dvn@speakandgetresults.com

ALLEN VAYSBERG
Owner
allen@allenvaysberg.com

KIT WELCHLIN
Owner
Welchlin Communication
Strategies
kit@welchlin.com

STEVE WILCOX
Consultant
Resultants For Business, Inc
steve@theresultants.com

DENISE LEE YOHN
Author of What Great Brands Do
http://deniseleeyohn.com

build
relationships

nurture
communities

strengthen
the workforce

Volunteer or
invest in literacy.

MINNESOTA
Literacy
COUNCIL

mnliteracy.org/volunteer
mnliteracy.org/donate